For Maria —

To ever-lasting, long standing
friendships; I will
treasure ours always!
love,
June

1/98

The
Kinship
of *Women*

Keep well this book and bear in mind

A constant friend is hard to find.

The Kinship of Women

A CELEBRATION OF
ENDURING FRIENDSHIP

PAT ROSS

Andrews and McMeel
A Universal Press Syndicate Company
Kansas City

Set in Sabon
Designed by Virginia Norey

For text and photo permissions, see p. 130

LIBRARY OF CONGRESS CATALOGING-IN-PUBLICATION DATA
Ross, Pat, 1943-
    The kinship of women : a celebration of enduring friendship / by Pat Ross
        p.   cm.
    Includes bibliographical references.
    ISBN 0-8362-2751-4 (hc)
    1. Photography of women.   2. Friendship—Pictorial works.
    3. Ross, Pat, 1943–   —Photograph collections.   I. Title.
TR681.W6R67   1997   96-45959
302.3′4′082—dc20   CIP

ATTENTION: SCHOOLS AND BUSINESSES
Andrews and McMeel books are available at quantity discounts
with bulk purchase for educational, business, or sales promotional use.
For information, please write to:
Special Sales Department,
Andrews and McMeel,
4250 Main Street, Kansas City, Missouri 64111.

For Leisa Crane

Irrepressible team captain and our dear friend

*Leisa (left) with Lisa Japy,
her friend from college*

Introduction

We simply cannot get on all that well
without each other.
⌐ Yet Another Anonymous Woman

Friendship among women threads through our lives and sustains us—so much so that many years later we find that even our earliest friendship memories have merely been tucked away for safekeeping. I feel that way when I remember my first *real* best friend, Barbara.

It was 1950, the dawning of what came to be called rock and roll, and the year I had the good fortune of living just four houses from Barbara Jackson. Television was a relatively new vice, and neither of our families approved. So Barbara and I were each other's entertainment, each other's commercial break. We played, we plotted, we shared, we endured.

We also watched through a wide crack in the bedroom door, stifling giggles, as Barbara's mother shimmied and squeezed her ample form into a Playtex Living Girdle that snapped into place like a giant rubber band. We read the secret love letters that her teenage brother hid in his messy sock drawer while, insult upon injury, we defiantly *touched* his brand-new Bill Haley and the Comets record. When the neighborhood bully rode back and forth on his bike looking for victims, we hid deep in the thick hydrangea bushes planted close to her modest white house and buried our faces in those gigantic cool pom-poms. Barbara's mother gave her one bad home permanent after another and eventually fried her thin brown hair. I lied each time and told her it looked pretty. When I got chicken pox, Barbara stood in the freezing cold below my bedroom window, shivering and waving and holding up the get-well card my class had made.

Then my family bought a house in a different school district. I refused to leave my friend, but the inevitable move took place, and somehow I got on with life. Back in the fifties, children didn't pick up the phone and call their friends, so Barbara and I lost each other. There have been other Barbaras since second grade, but to this day I cannot pass hydrangeas in full bloom without remembering my first best friend.

This book began with a handful of old photographs of American women—

individual studio portraits as well as women together—that I had been drawn to collecting. I enjoyed pondering the histories of these anonymous images, especially the ones that showed the moods and faces of female friendship: best friends, groups of friends, community gatherings. In the beginning, my selections were made by a kind of whimsical radar, for I had no particular goal in mind. But my personal standard insisted that the images must clearly communicate an immediate unspeakable bond, declaring, "Yes, there we are!" Ultimately, it didn't matter if we knew who these women were; they were we.

At first, I'd pick up odd photos at garage sales and flea markets. Then I hit the big time when I discovered ephemera (meaning anything old on paper) shows, picture postcard bonanzas, and urbane dealers at photography exhibitions. Over nearly a decade, my modest collection outgrew a small shoe box and became more official in its own cardboard file, always pulling at my

sleeve to become a book. That's when my search became more organized and more discriminating. The photographer in me went for strong composition; the feminist in me sought spirit and resilience; the mother in me scanned faces for compassion; the friend in me found humor and companionship.

Many of the postwar photographs—too "new" for dealers to consider valuable—came from friends who happily sifted through family albums and stacks of faded memories, revisiting the past with their mothers, sisters, daughters, college roommates, and other friends for life. Many thanked me for asking them for this favor. Perhaps a few too many photographs came from my own family albums, for I could not resist the shot of my pretty young mother with her neighborhood friends, so proudly holding their babies up for the camera; my sweet grandmother and her friends lounging playfully on the grass in their Victorian whites; my spirited daughter Erica as a young girl making muscles with her friend; Aunt Jerri, my earliest mentor, frolicking in the surf with women who remained her friends for life; and, finally, a snapshot of my adoring little sister Jeanne, whose bicycle today seems symbolically overshadowed by mine.

It seemed fitting to use the photographs in an anthology with words by women only, taken from their journals, autobiographies, short stories, novels, essays, and poetry. The selections come from the same broad span of time as the photographs—from the mid-1800s to the present day. At the start, I assumed that the more historic voices would be matched with the vintage shots, and the more contemporary writers would best complement the more contemporary images. And sometimes this was the case. But in other instances, I was proven wrong when a thoroughly irreverent nineteenth-century voice perfectly suited an up-to-date snapshot. Happily, the reflections of most of the writers in *The Kinship of Women* are universal and inter-changeable. When all the texts and photos were matched, I felt that many of the more "unlikely" pairings showed rather poignantly that the nature of women's friendship hasn't really changed much over the years.

A book on women's friendship that begins with the earliest years and comes full circle spans many ages and stages and hence countless possibilities for dividing a lifetime. I chose three distinct parts that seem to show how female friendship evolves.

The Kinship of Women opens quite simply with the formative friend-ships that are our "beginnings." Thrown together in school situations and neighborhood surroundings, our childhood friends are a lot like us in most respects. In writer Jamaica Kincaid's words we are "joined at the shoulder, hip, ankle, not to mention heart." When our horizons expand to high school and then college, our friendships expand too. According to Victorian manners

authority Margaret Sangster, we hold fast to our early "sweet associations." Lucy Larcom, a per-ceptive nineteenth-century writer, saw fit to men-tion that we are good at "exchanging confi-dences" at any age. The so-called gossip and trivia are actually the special way our sex exchanges viewpoints and shares perceptions of the world. Girls and women become more authentic through their friends. Whether we share lipstick or knowledge, the early friendships remain etched in our memory.

"Validations" finds women out in the

world—with partners, children, job demands, and myriad commitments. Now more than ever, we need friends to share our common interests, our daily joys and sorrows. We need women friends who support us and say, "I feel the very same way." When our busy lives threaten to rob us of our friends, we work hard to fit them in. According to Elsa Walsh, we crave "the rich intimate territory of women's talk" to make us laugh, find empathy with our life's stories, and keep us from reaching the end of our collective ropes. Around the quilting frame or over cappuccino, women have done what women do so well: they talk, share, communicate, confirm.

One sure way to bring women together in full voice is a just cause. In the late sixties, I discovered the newly emerging Women's Movement and embraced it wholeheartedly. As a fledgling editor of children's books, I saw inequity there and soon joined with other women to do something about it. We became official: Feminists on Children's Media, a group of young profes-sional women from New York City and a group of young mothers from suburban New Jersey, joined by some rather curious but effective net-working. Our mission was to expose stereotyped images of girls and women, as well as boys and men, in children's books and other media. We worked together with commitment and fervor and eventually made a difference, which is exact-ly what we had set out to do. But in the process, we made a difference to one another as well. We became friends and confidants—a community. We learned to trust each other in new ways.

When my daughter Erica was born in 1972, the collective group sent a baby gift—the smallest size baseball glove. It sat in its box next to pink organdy dresses and adorable dolls. The comments about the baseball glove ranged from "Did somebody think you had a boy?" to "I don't get it." But I got it. And at that time in my life, I saw that little baseball glove as one of the most beautiful, supportive messages in the world.

I hold a particular bias for the third stage of friendship—"Reflections"—for that is where I am today. "The gold friend knows all of your past dirt and glories," writes Jill McCorkle. Time seasons the meaning of friendship. Eventually we come to appreciate these relationships as durable and fragile at the same time, so we value them even more. Even our gifts are simpler and more relevant: a loaf of home-baked bread, bath crystals, warm socks, a wooden spoon, a hardcover copy of a well-chosen book like *What I Wore,* or the latest "Meditations for Women Who Do Too Much" calendar. Writer and women's scholar Louise Bernikow speaks of these meaningful gifts as "a laying on of hands." Years may come between us, yet we can pick up in the middle of a sentence and feel as though no time has lapsed at all.

"May we grow in age as we grow in grace." This is the motto of St. Margaret's, a girls' boarding school where I made friendships that have lasted through shipwrecked marriages and renewed vows, wayward children and high achievers, Prozac and estrogen, prestigious awards and dubious distinction, coming out and coming back, near-poverty and vast inheritance, high-profile accomplishment and contented obscurity. When I was a student there, the idea of growing in grace fell on deaf ears. Yet grace is indeed an integral part of female friendship. My thesaurus gives thirty-one alternate words for "grace," among them ease, balance, goodness, compassion, blessing, and praise. Ultimately, it's this combined grace that distinguishes the completion stage of women's friendship.

In the end, a spirited and moving blend of over seventy women's images and voices celebrates connections made at playgrounds, quilting bees, kitchen sinks, beauty salons, park benches, baby showers, coffee machines, and other familiar places where women have traditionally gathered. These words and images move forward as women have moved forward, into workplaces and more contemporary circumstances where friendship continues. When all is said and done, the sentiments range from warm and insightful to funny and irreverent—much like the women friends I have come to treasure.

Beginnings

The companions of our childhood always
possess a certain power over our minds which
hardly any later friend can obtain.

— Mary Shelley,
1818

Mary Virginia German hugging Patsy Kienzle—early best friends in Baltimore, Maryland, 1947.

We'd set off for school side by side, our feet in step, not touching but feeling as if we were joined at the shoulder, hip, ankle, not to mention heart.

— Jamaica Kincaid,
1983

I went to tea at Elizabeth's house,
    And what did she serve but tea!
I sat as still as a well-bred mouse
When I went to tea at Elizabeth's house.
I didn't snarl and I didn't grouse
Though I was distressed to see
That tea at my friend Elizabeth's house
Meant absolutely tea.

              — Margaret Fishback
                (1904–1985)

A *thousand sweet associations* dating back
to the scarcely remembered days of infancy
twine themselves in with a sisterly friendship.

— Margaret E. Sangster,
1906

hey looked at me and across me in every direction with rich, gleeful, gentle eyes. They were merry, loud, quarrelsome and loving; they showed off, had tantrums, gabbled and slapped each other; they called and murmured to me; their soiled, perspiring fingers fondled my hands. I felt a wonderful sense of home among them. Their collective presence was like honey.

—Sarah N. Cleghorn, 1936
on her work with the girls at
St. Stephen's Church
New York City

*Amanda Cameron and Leigh Anne Cameron in their great-grandmother's garden
at "Inverness," Gordonsville, Virginia, 1987.*

Girls especially are fond of exchanging confidences with those who they think they can trust; it is one of the most charming traits of a simple, earnest-hearted girlhood, and they are the happiest women who never lose it entirely.

—Lucy Larcom,
1889

The flat roof of an apartment house, or the lawn, yard, or open field about a private house, is accessible to nearly every group of young girls who would be benefitted physically by a happy little dance together in the open air.

—Mary A. Laselle,
1914

*Image reproduced from
an early tintype.*

For there is no friend like a sister

In calm or stormy weather;

To cheer one on the tedious way,

To fetch one if one goes astray,

To lift one if one totters down,

To strengthen while one stands.

—Christina Rossetti,
1862

At sixteen and until we married, Doris and I were totally together. We dressed alike until the day I got married, which sounds ridiculous. At the age of twenty-two, on the way to my wedding, we were dressed alike! We look at it now and just laugh.

— Naomi Cohen
(b. 1924)

*An all-day community sing and supper
in Pie Town, New Mexico, June 1940.*

I think both [Aunt] Hannah and [Aunt] Jenny were virgins, but if they were, there were no signs of spinsterhood. They were nice about married people, they were generous to children, and sex was something to have fun about. Jenny had been the consultant to many neighborhood young ladies before their marriage night, or the night of their first lover. One of these girls, a rich ninny, Jenny found irritating and unpleasant. When I was sixteen I came across the two of them in earnest conference on the lawn, and later Jenny told me that the girl had come to consult her about how to avoid pregnancy.

"What did you tell her?"

"I told her to have a glass of ice water right before the sacred act and three sips during it."

When we had finished laughing, I said, "But she'll get pregnant."

"He's marrying her for money, he'll leave her when he gets it. This way at least maybe she'll have a few babies for herself."

And four years later, when I wrote my aunts that I was going to be married, I had back a telegram:

FORGET ABOUT THE GLASS OF ICE WATER, TIMES HAVE CHANGED.

—Lillian Hellman,
1969

Some people we can always depend upon for making the best, instead of the worst, of whatever happens. For we all of us have some friends, or friend, to whom we instinctively carry every one of our griefs or vexations, assured that if any one can help us, they can and will.

—Anonymous Woman Writer,
1858

Friends at the
Mary E. Scott Chinese Sunday School,
First Baptist Church, Philadelphia,
Pennsylvania, 1932.

*T*o *have a mother who loves you* for being independent is to have a mother who fosters rebellion in your heart and revolution in your bones.

—Judy Chicago,
1975

Jennifer Usdan (left) and Erica Ross,
born two days apart in November of 1972.

*T*he soul selects her own society.

—Emily Dickinson
(1830–1886)

Esther Goldberg (right)
poses with her friend in
Massachusetts, 1930

Written on the back: No 1 is Bertha La Vaie,
student nurse at Melrose Hospital, others are her cousins.

My heart has just been called back to the time when we used to sit with our arms around each other at the sunset hour & talk of our friends & our homes & of ten thousand subjects of mutual interest until both our hearts felt warmer & lighter for the pure communion of spirit.

—Antoinette Brown to Lucy Stone

I've always been a jock, long before it was fashionable for women to be running around in exercise suits. But for most of my life it wasn't easy to find athletic women, and I was somewhat self-conscious about it. I never did give it up, though, and I was always looking for friends to do athletic things with. Like I said, they were hard to find, so when I found them, they were like a treasure.

—Anonymous Woman

The mood of a reunion is fond. That's what it is: *fond.* Like a strawberry dipped to the stem in warm chocolate, you will be immersed in kindness and come away coated with it.

—Melinda Worth Popham,
1994

Having tea in a college dormitory room.

LENORE SIMON (Len - G. in the snapshot) REMEMBERS:

Our group *The Fireflies* (also called The Coquettes) lived in the West Bronx. Our colors were to be cerulean blue and burnt sienna, but we never got around to the jackets. We all attended public school 86. We formed our little club at ages 13–14 & got together frequently—roller skating around the Reservoir, going to the movies together, the Big Band Shows at Radio City Music Hall & lots of sojourns to the Bronx Zoo & Botanical Gardens—accessible by a Trolley Ride. We collected dues & used our collection toward occasional parties—all non-alcoholic beverages. Wildest activity—Spin the Bottle! And we had lots of fun— Dancing to Record Player Music—Our most daring exploit—cutting H.S. to see and hear the Big Bands. Hazel had a big crush on Singer Bob Eberle (who died not too long ago) & saved his crushed cigarette!—I can recall Danny Kaye performing at one show—& asking those in the audience who were playing hooky to stand up! As we did, the lights in the theater came on—And in momentary horror, we thought we'd be hauled away by truant officers.

College chemistry class, turn of the century.

I *have such an intense pride* of sex that
the triumphs of women in art, literature,
oratory, science, or song rouse my enthusiasm as
nothing else can.

—Elizabeth Cady Stanton,
1898

I *knew as our senior year was drawing* to a close that we were about to experience a great loss. Oh sure, we'd always be there for each other; we'd live on the telephone. But what about the way we told each other everything that happened? What about the jokes other people didn't think were funny because they hadn't been in that seventh-grade classroom? What about our great album collection?

But there was no need to worry. We are still taping albums to fill in the gaps. Now we talk and tell everything that has happened during the week. We call to complain ("the baby has an ear infection" or "it's too damn hot to go outside"); to get reassurance ("who has time to just lie around in the sun and get skin cancer?"); to get that totally biased opinion that we all need from time to time (she always reads all of my work in manuscript); or simply to gossip (between the two of us we know all of the hometown news even though neither of us lives there. . . .) We have huge phone bills but we always rationalize that they aren't as much as an hour with a really good shrink.

—Jill McCorkle,
1994

*Students celebrating a 1985 national news article
about their all-women's school.*

*O*nly *by becoming friends with* other women, by understanding what we share—and don't share—can we truly begin to know what it is to be a woman today. Women friends can help us to see through the myths and misconceptions that still characterize our thinking about women today. By nurturing those aspects of our nature that are distinctly female, they can also help us to value the women in ourselves.

Because men have been more highly valued in our society, we must guard against seeing our women friends as second rate, mere understudies to be cast aside when the male star arrives. Although it's possible to have good male friends, it's worth remembering that male-centered women are vulnerable to not getting their own needs met, for as a rule, it is women, not men, who nurture other women.

—Judith Finlayson,
1993

Every good woman needs a companion of her own sex. No matter how numerous or valuable her acquaintances, if she has a genial, loving nature, the want of a female friend is felt as a sad void.

— Georgina Bruce Kirby
writing in her diary,
February 3, 1853

*T*o *understand the splendor of* the women of the Renaissance, it is not necessary to be a student of history. One has but to turn to Shakespeare to know these women in the flesh. Beatrice, Portia, Rosalind, Isabel, Viola, Constance—brave and witty, executive and adventurous, saintly and ardent, agonized and enduring—they give us the perfume of that glowing time as no historian can hope to do. So successful are they, so enterprising, that it has been said that in the twentieth century Shakespeare would undoubtedly have been a suffragist—and perhaps a militant!

—Beatrice Forbes-Robertson Hale,
1914

*M*any an unmarried girl is blind to the virtues of women because she has not time to study them. Her horizon is bound by masculine forms, and she is quite content to have it so. By and by, when she concentrates her attention and interest on one man and the others disappear like setting stars at the rise of the sun, why then she notices the beauty and fragrance of those human flowers—women.

—Ella Wheeler Wilcox,
1893

At noon they walked downtown and looked in the windows of a beautiful carpeted store that sold only wedding and evening clothes. Anita planned a springtime wedding, with bridesmaids in pink-and-green silk and overskirts of white organza. Margot's wedding was to take place in the fall, with the bridesmaids wearing apricot velvet. In Woolworth's they looked at lipsticks and earrings. They dashed into the drugstore and sprayed themselves with sample cologne. If they had any money to buy some necessity for their mothers, they spent some of the change on cherry Cokes or sponge toffee. They could never be deeply unhappy, because they believed that something remarkable was bound to happen to them. They could become heroines; love and power of some sort were surely waiting.

—Alice Munro,
1990

Anita Kienzle with Patsy (far left) and other mothers
and babies in Baltimore, Maryland, 1943.

Few comforts are more alluring for a woman than the rich intimate territory of women's talk. A woman friend will say, "You are not alone. I have felt that way, too. This is what happened to me." Home, in other words.

— Elsa Walsh,
1994

*M*otherhood, *daughterhood, sisterhood* and friendship are simple terms that cannot adequately describe the nature of the complex relationships that they name. . . . For many women, past and present, diaries serve an important function: they help to weave the threads of such relationships into the fabric of women's experience as part of the domestic ritual that women continue to create daily.

—Penelope Franklin,
1980

Photo dated June 1, 1909.

*S*o *closely interwoven* have been our lives,
  our purposes and experiences that, separated,
we have a feeling of incompleteness—united,
such strength of self-association that no ordinary
obstacles, difficulties or danger ever appear to us
as insurmountable.

— Elizabeth Cady Stanton
writing about Susan B. Anthony, 1898

*I*t is good to be a woman today. In every land our sisters are stirring, feeling the prickings of their growing wings, lifting their hands to the sun. As a sex women are alive in the world as never before. They are learning the great lesson of cooperation, which has enabled men to win continents. They are learning sex-loyalty.

— Beatrice Forbes-Robertson Hale,
1914

Billed as "Versatility Without Mediocrity," the Maurer Sisters (shown above and on facing page) traveled as part of the Chatauqua organization. Frances (far left, above) played the coronet and did humorous readings and imitations. Edith played the flute and doubled with fancy whistling and birdcalls. Gladys, the youngest, played the violin. The oldest sister, Inez, played the piano.

*W*hether *we have sisters* or not,
we look for the archetype of the sister;
the woman who knows us better than anyone,
who shares everything with us, who loves us as
a blood relation.

— Carmen Renee Berry and
Tamara Traeder,
1995

Why have men always possessed an exclusive right to a sense of humor? I believe it is because they live out-of-doors more. Humor is an out-of-doors virtue. It requires ozone and the light of the sun. And when the new woman came out-of-doors to live and mingled with men and newer women, she saw funny things, and her sense of humor began to grow and thrive.

The fun of the situation is entirely lost if you stay at home too much.

—Lilian Bell,
1897

Evelin Antoinette Sis   once
     Olivia   Eve

We'll all be better off when word gets around that cleaning a toilet produces no more and no less than a clean toilet; it does not produce strength of character, nor is it interesting work.

—Gabrielle Burton,
1976

She is generous, funny, kind, brilliant, non-judgmental, and she has the greatest collection of shoes I have ever seen.

—Connie Porter,
1994

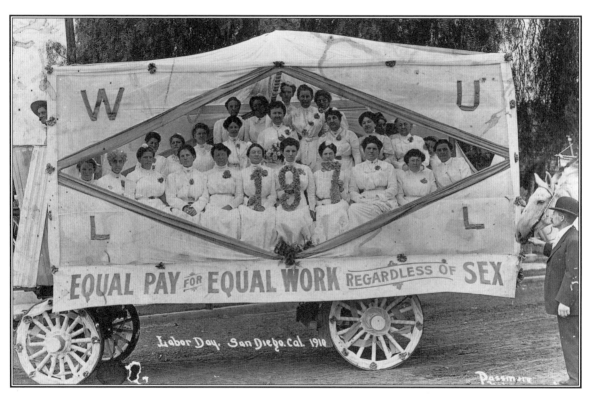

The Women's Union Label League #197 float in
the 1910 Labor Day Parade, San Diego, California.

*T*he newest and strongest power of the age has been engendered through organizations of women.

—Haryot Holt Cahoon,
1893

For women there are, undoubtedly, great difficulties in the path, but so much the more to overcome. First, no woman should say, "I am but a woman!" But a woman! What more can you ask to be?

—Maria Mitchell,
1874

*T*alk *between* women friends
is always therapy. . . .

→ Jayne Anne Phillips,
1994

A "drinking bee" at White Chapel, Dawson, Alaska.

*T*wo may talk together under the same roof for many years yet never really meet; and two others at first speech are old friends.

→Mary Catherwood
(1847–1902)

*Written in pencil
on the back:*
Yetta and Ethel.

*I*n conclusion, all I can say is "Talk! Talk! Talk!" We are more moved by one conversation than by many eloquent discourses. After all, what is so permanently delightful as communion of ideas?

—Florence Farr,
1910

Written on the back: Cutting Room, Mutual Fabrick Co., Nov. 1928.

I want you to go down into this common everyday drudgery . . . and consider if there might not be in it also a great warfare.

—Rebecca Harding Davis,
1861

It's never too late to be what you
might have become.

—George Eliot
(1819–1880)

Rodeo cowgirls circa 1920.

I *am part of a process,* a community of women. As we move beyond the old social norms with our new visions and support systems, we will experience the joy that comes from being seekers.

→Judith Finlayson,
1993

𝒰nderstand that *friendship arrives* from the least likely sources and flourishes in the least likely locations. Understand that someone can know you very well though you have not told her about yourself.

—Whitney Otto,
1994

*Roberta Emery fixes the hair of her friend and
neighbor, Etta Mae McKee, at the local grocery store in
Pie Town, New Mexico, June 1940, where Etta Mae works.
The nearest beauty shop is some eighty miles away.*

A Tupperware party circa 1953.

*D*oris's daughter gave a Mary Kay Cosmetic Party today. There were hot cinnamon rolls and coffee. The demonstrator passed out palettes of paint and foul-smelling oils. She said they were secret lotions invented by a tanner in Illinois to turn tough, large-pored hides into kid gloves. Diane, the wrangler on this ranch, had never used make-up before. The lotion floated on her face like grease over gravy.

As the woman demonstrated, her eight-month-old baby sat on the hearth and quietly ate a pot of rouge. The woman said it was her ambition to move to Colorado and sell so many products the company gave her a pink Cadillac with *Mary Kay* stenciled on the door. Painted up, we stepped out into the gray afternoon. Doris yelled over her shoulder, "Well, I'm off to feed the chickens." We were steaming with gardenia perfume.

—Sandra Alcosser,
1977

We rode a day, from east to west,
     To meet. A year had done its best
By absence, and by loss of speech,
To put beyond the other's reach
Each heart and life.
But, drawing nigh,
"Ah! It is you!"
"Yes, it is I!"

—Helen Hunt Jackson
(1819–1880)

PART THREE

Reflections

The silver friend knows your present and the
gold friend knows all of your past dirt and
glories. Once in a blue moon there's someone
who knows it all, someone who knows and
accepts you unconditionally, someone who's
there for life.

— Jill McCorkle,
1996

A summer's night on an avenue crowded with restaurants. The man walking beside me observes the great numbers of women out for the evening together. I have ceased to think of this as remarkable. I have come to think of this as a period in history, like one or two others, in which women find each other the most interesting people around, in which women find new thinking, new ways of looking at the world, in other women far more than they do in men. I have come to feel my own life as one in which women are an enormous delight, at least most of the women I know, and that to cancel an appointment with a woman because a man had called would not only violate my own expectations and hers, but it is unthinkable and would diminish my life.

—Louise Bernikow,
1980

Elizabeth Gore (foreground) and Mary Lou Butler,
northern neck of Virginia, 1970.

Most women would agree. Our friends are among life's greatest treasures. They help us negotiate the difficult hurdles of life. What would we have done without friends in adolescence to help us navigate the travails of puberty and deal with our "unreasonable" parents? And what about our twentysomething romances? Whom do we go to for emotional rescue when in the dating years the man of our dreams becomes the stuff of nightmares? We go to our friends. Later, they coach us through first-time motherhood. Years later as we help our kids pack for college, they witness our tears. Our friends walk with us through menopause as, once again, we are caught up in the hormonal crazies, and they listen as we fantasize about fleeing to the Caribbean or a convent.

In their presence, we laugh about what drove us crazy hours before; with them we cry without shame, knowing we will be understood.

—Brenda Hunter,
1994

*B*y the time this is published, Jackie Joseph and I will both be sixty. We will have been . . . close friends, best friends, for forty-seven years. I've gotten fat; Jackie's deaf in one ear. But I don't see that we've changed much.

—Carolyn See,
1994

Betty Stephens (right) with her friend Bertha Simmons,
posing together in a photo booth, 1932.

Dear Donna,

When I returned home from the Saturday walk with you along the river, I enjoyed recalling how freely we had laughed with each other. Did you notice that? It was a lighthearted afternoon just because I felt so easy with you, so sure.

I can risk showing you my eccentricities, knowing full well that—amazingly—nothing has ever shaken your trust in my basic integrity. Your respect and unquestioned support of me throughout the years has confirmed me in my most vulnerable moments—too bitter or fragile to share with anyone except for you. Often wordless and purely intuitive, our friendship is a precious gift I carry with me weightlessly, thankfully . . . .

—Eugenia,
1994

*M*y mother and I were very, very good friends. I enjoyed her company. After my father died, for seven years I was there every single day. I ate there. I slept there. I'd go home and clean up my house and come back. I used to come and stay. There wasn't any reason why I shouldn't. I knew that my mother didn't like to be alone. I think originally I thought I'd go over for a week and I stayed for seven and a half years.

—Belle Stock
(b. 1913)

Elisa Foster (76) and her daughter,
Viola Nesbitt (62)—May 28, 1970.

I *still get choked up* when I think of my grandmother. She meant so much to me. . . . Sometimes we stayed with her for a week, or for a night, or for a holiday. She wanted me to have shiny hair. Once she washed my hair with an egg; another time it was vinegar. She played a very significant role in my life. . . .

My mother and I are very, very close. I tell her everything. We think in a similar way. I didn't expect to be different from my mother and my grandmother. I saw how similar they were to each other, and I expected to be the same. In some ways my life is so different. . . . Still, I am similar in very basic ways.

—Ruth Zober
(b. 1949)

I imagine a group of fishermen's wives sitting in a circle a hundred years ago and sewing these small scraps of color into a perfectly integrated whole that somehow suggests the moods of Nantucket. We will take this quilt home as a token of the house to come, of nights when we will listen to real waves breaking on our own small piece of beach and be kept warm by their namesake.

—Linda Pastan,
1977

Every woman who makes of her living something strong and good is sharing bread with us.

—Marge Piercy
(b. 1936)

These unidentified women were traveling together on a train trip in 1922 from New York City to Portland, Oregon, with stops at national parks and major cities along the way.

I *spend the afternoon with* two women friends, Carol and Barlow. We haven't been together for perhaps six months or more. It was as if our conversation started again in midsentence. As if we were just coming back into the room after a trip to the kitchen to get something out of the refrigerator. We were speaking to some part of ourselves that has a continuity of its own. A part that is switched off as we go about our separate lives, but when we are together we tune in the same channel and continue the program. Several times during the afternoon one of them said, "God, I've been starving for this conversation."

—Eleanor Coppola,
1980

I*ntensity* commands form.

—May Sarton
(1912–1995)

Exercise class in Park Forest, Illinois,
one of the country's first suburbs, 1953.

*O*ne friend and I have been through a marriage apiece,
reams of gossip and countless conversations about the difficulty
of finding a decent lipstick. Yet in the end, we always come back to our
work. Work is our passion, its language our language, and if we have
both maintained our footing on some rather perilous ladders, I believe
we owe our stubborn balance as much to each other as to ourselves.

—Mary Cantwell,
1996

*Frances Hafner and Nellie Tannenbaum circa 1935—piano partners
and musicians from Brooklyn, New York, who met in middle age and
went on to fame and notoriety, giving concerts on radio station
WNYC every Sunday morning for nearly eight years.*

Any woman who sews
or knits, or weaves,
blends colors in a tapestry
or creates a patchwork quilt,
knows by the feel
that a single thread is weak
but the weaving,
the blending,
the intertwining
with many others
makes it strong.

Any woman alone,
without friends
to sustain her,
to nurture and support,
to hold with loving arms,
like a single thread, is weak.
But the weaving,
the loving,
the nurturing of others,
the networks of friendship
makes her strong.

— "Barbara,"
1994

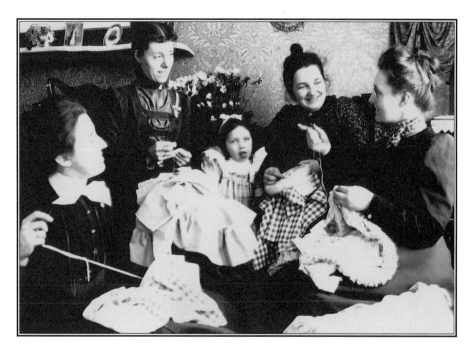

Jotted on the back: Ginny White, Lillie Geiger, Dorothy Presbury, Charlotte Presbury, Mary Lincoln.

We have just had our present-giving at Alice's, just we three old girls. Alice's house was full of the smell of new bread. The loaves were piled on the kitchen table; the dining-room table was piled with parcels, things changing hands. This is our system and it works well: we agree on a stated amount—it is small because our big giving is birthdays. Each of us buys something for ourselves to our own liking, goods amounting to the stated sums. We bring them along and Christmas Eve, with kissings and thankings, accept them from each other—homely, practical little wants, torch batteries, hearth brooms, coffee strainers, iron handles, etc. It's lots of fun. We lit four red candles in the window and drank ginger ale and ate Christmas cake and new bread and joked and discussed today and tomorrow and yesterday and compared tirednesses and rheumatics and rejoiced that Christmas came only once per year. We love each other, we three; with all our differences we are very close.

—Emily Carr,
Christmas Eve, 1935

NOT THE HEN HOUSE

The yackety-yak and the laughter
Is not the clucking of hens,
But the turning of keys in locks
The withdrawal of bolts
Experience freed,
The coming together of souls.

The yeast is fermenting now
Leavening our tomorrows,
And safe in the lives of women
The wine will be slowly maturing.

—Irene Smythe,
1994

Water Aerobics in Yuma,
Arizona, 1986.

*A photograph on an old postcard, the message
faded and illegible, addressed to someone in Illinois.*

I *had an old friend* who happened to fancy, as accessories to a costume in which to pass her declining years, a bustle and a certain false front. Bustles went their way, and a few people still clung to them; then even the faithful gave them up, but my friend still wore hers valiantly. It suited her to do so. . . .

None who loved her, and they were many, would have had her altered in any respect. There was but one exception to this—her widowed daughter, who with her little girls made her home with her mother. The bustle and false front caused her the keenest pain. I do not believe my friend ever got herself ready for a party without her daughter trying to decrease the size of that bustle. . . .

I am glad to relate that my old friend wore her bustle, her daughter notwithstanding, almost to her dying day. I hope they buried it with her—she made a brave fight for it. She is to me an inspiring memory.

—Anonymous Woman Writer,
1911

You *can* *date* *the* *evolving* *life* of a mind,
like the age of a tree, by the rings of friendship formed by the expanding central trunk.

—Mary McCarthy,
1987

Playing checkers with bottle caps.

*W*hen a great adventure is offered,
you don't refuse it.

—Amelia Earhart
(1897–1937)

Kitty Tatch and her friend cavort high above
Yosemite Valley sometime during 1900. It is said
that Kitty used to autograph this photograph for friends
and guests at a nearby hotel where she was a waitress.

As I recall the throngs of unknown girlish forms that used to pass and repass me on the familiar road to the mill gates, and also the few that I knew so well—those with whom I worked, thought, read, wrote, studied, and worshiped—my thoughts sent a heartfelt greeting to them all, wherever in God's beautiful, busy universe they may now be scattered: "I am glad I have lived in the world with you!"

—Lucy Larcom,
1889

For Friendship's Sake

The complex yet sustaining journey from the first photgraphs to a finished book has involved many wonderful associates, good friends, and special family members. The list may look a bit like a crowd scene, but each of you means something special to me. My project-related friends include my smart and thoughtful editor Chris Schillig at Andrews and McMeel and her fine staff; the very best researchers, Leisa Crane, Judy Gitenstein, Priya Wadhera, and Gillian Speeth; my agent Elaine Markson; and the book's talented designer Virginia Norey. Appreciation to Margaret Broad and Sue Semsch at St. Margaret's School; and to Shirley Peterson, Pamela Zusi, and Joy Derr at Hood College. Other indispensible associates included Carol Hedges and Bob Krueger at Time Frame and the staff at Crawford-Doyle Books.

Last but not least, there are my sustaining friends of both genders: Joan Bell, Jane Bergere, Laurel Blossom, Carlie Collier, Nancy Coplon, Charles Crane, Maryann Foster, Charlotte Frischkorn, Moira Garvey, Carolyn Gore-Ashe and her mother Elizabeth Gore, Betsy Gould, Margie Haber, Marilyn Hafner, Nancy Hays, Gene Heil, Lee Bennett Hopkins, Patty Laufer and her mother Esther Jonas, Joslin Leonardson, Charles Muise, Arlene Raven, Margaret Ray, Gail Rock, Marsha Schmidt, Mary Semple, Meri Stevens, Joan Suyhada, Leonard Todd, and Gigi Zimmer.

The love and support so consistently offered by my mother Anita Kienzle, my sister Jeane Kienzle, my aunt Jerri Fowler, and my partner Ken McGraw went well beyond an inscribed gratitude. This makes up my own kinship of friends and family.

Photo Credits

The following photographs, indicated by the page on which they appear, have been printed with permission: v: courtesy Charles Crane; viii: courtesy Time Frame; x: courtesy Joslin Leonardson; 6 and 10: photos by Carlie Collier, courtesy Carlie Collier; 11: Roy Andrews Special Collection, University of Oregon Library; 13, 67, 97, and 119: Urban Archives, Temple University, Philadelphia, Pennsylvania; 18 and 81: photos by Russell Lee, courtesy The Library of Congress; 21: Balch Institute for Ethnic Studies Library; 24: courtesy Esther Jonas; xiii, 29, and 37: St. Margaret's School Archives; 33: photo and text courtesy Lenore Simon; 30, 34, 38, and 106: Hood College Archives; 55: JANEART; 56 and 57: courtesy Gene Heil; 64: San Diego Historical Society, Photograph Collection; 68: Alaska Historical Library, Larss and Duchlos Collection; 77: Buffalo Bill Historical Center, Cody, Wyoming; 82: Archive Photos; 90 and 104: courtesy Elizabeth Gore; 94: Courtesy of Lane County Historical Museum; 107: photo by Dan Weiner, courtesy Sandra Weiner; 108: photo courtesy Marylin Hafner; 115: photo by David Graham, courtesy David Graham; 120: LeRoy Radanovich, Radanovich Photography.

Women & Friendship
Sources

This bibliography contains a selection of noteworthy and accessible contemporary books that contributed significantly to the text (references follow entries). Grateful appreciation to publishers, literary agents, and authors who so helpfully gave me permission to reprint from their works.

Bernikow, Louise. *Among Women*. New York: Harper & Row, 1981. (Page 88). Reprinted with permission of the author.

Berry, Carmen Renee and Tamara Traeder. *Girlfriends: Invisible Bonds, Enduring Ties*. Berkeley, California: Wildcat Canyon Press, 1995. © 1995 by Carmen Renee Berry and Tamara C. Traeder. (Page 57). Reprinted with permission of the authors and publisher.

Biggs, Mary. *Women's Words: The Columbia Book of Quotations by Women*. New York: Columbia University Press, 1996. (Pages 102 and 118).

Cantwell, Mary. "Lawless Friendship." New York: *The New York Times "Lives"* column, March 17, 1996. (Page 109).

Chicago, Judy. *Through the Flower: My Struggle As a Woman Artist*. New York: Doubleday & Company, 1975. (Page 23).

Finlayson, Judith. *The New Woman's Diary*. New York: Crown Publishers, Inc., 1993. © 1993 Judith Finlayson. (Pages 39, 61, 79). Reprinted with permission of the publisher.

Franklin, Penelope. *Private Pages: Diaries of American Women*. New York: Ballantine Books, 1980. (Page 50).

Hellman, Lillian. *An Unfinished Woman*. Boston: Little, Brown & Company, 1969. © 1969 Lillian Hellman. (Page 19). Reprinted with permission of the publisher.

Hen Co-op. *Growing Old Disgracefully*. Freedom, California: The Crossing Press, 1994. (Pages 110 and 114). Reprinted with permission of the publisher.

Hunter, Brenda. *In The Company of Women*. Portland, Oregon: Multnomah Books, 1994. © 1994 Brenda Hunter, Ph. D. (Pages 49, 91).

Kincaid, Jamaica. *Annie John*. New York: Penguin U.S.A., 1986. (Page 3).

Krause, Corinne A. *Grandmothers, Mothers, and Daughters: Oral Histories of Three Generations of Ethnic American Women*. (Pages 16, 96, and 98) Excerpted with permission of Twayne Publishers, an imprint of Simon & Schuster MacMillan, © 1991 G.K. Hall & Co.

Lifshin, Lyn. *Ariadne's Thread*. New York: Harper & Row, 1982. (Pages 83, 101, and 105). Reprinted with permission of the individual authors.

Merriam, Eve. *Growing Up Female in America: Ten Lives*. Garden City, N.Y.: Doubleday & Co., 1971. (Page 66).

Moffat, Mary Jane and Charlotte Painter. *Revelations: Diaries of Women*. New York: Random House, Inc., 1974. (Page 113). Emily Carr excerpt from *Hundreds and Thousands*, Toronto, Vancouver: Clarke, Irwin & Co., 1966.

Munro, Alice. *Friends of My Youth*. New York: Alfred A. Knopf, 1990. © 1990 Alice Munro. (Page 46). Reprinted with permission of the publisher.

Norris, Gloria, ed.. *The Seasons of Women: An Anthology*. New York: W.W. Norton & Company, 1996. (Pages 36, 87). Jill McCorkle quotes from "Cathy, Now and Then," 1994 by Jill McCorkle. Reprinted with permission of Darhansoff & Verrill Literary Agency.

Otto, Whitney. *How to Make an American Quilt.* New York: Villard Books, 1994. (Page 80).

Pearlman, Mickey, ed. *Between Friends.* Boston: Houghton Mifflin Co., 1994 (Pages 31, 62, 69, and 92). Melinda Worth Popham quote from "Stripes," © 1994 Melinda Worth Popham; Connie Porter quote from "GirlGirlGirl," © 1994 Connie Porter; Jayne Anne Phillips quote from "Road Trip: The Real Thing," © 1994 Jayne Anne Phillips; Carolyn See quote from "Best Friend, My Wellspring in the Wilderness!" © 1994 by Carolyn See.

Rubin, Lillian B. *Just Friends: The Role of Friendship in Our Lives.* New York: Harper & Row, 1985. (Page 28).

Wartenberg, Eugenia. 1994. Permission of the author for use of private letter. (Page 95).

Pat Ross (right) with Jeanne Kienzle,
her sister and friend for life, 1954.

About the Author

Pat Ross began collecting vintage photographs of women a number of years ago as a hobby and soon discovered a book idea in her collection. She is the author of the best-selling *Formal Country* as well as *Remembering Main Street,* a book featuring more than a hundred of her own photographs of small-town life. Pat Ross's longtime involvement in women's issues, dating back to her active participation in the Women's Movement and the 1970 publication of her first book for young adults entitled *Young and Female: Turning Points in the Lives of Eight American Women,* were stepping stones to *The Kinship of Women.* The author of more than thirty books for adults and children, Pat Ross divides her time between an apartment in New York City and a farm in rural Virginia, a lifestyle she calls "culture shock both ways and the perfect balance."